I0621503

The Great
RESCUE

This story is dedicated to pet parents across the globe.

Thanks to you, there are many more "Graysons" that have a happy story to share.

Pughearts
Houston Pug Rescue
www.pughearts.com

100% of profits from this book go directly to PugHearts. Thank you.

Title
The Great Rescue - Grayson's Story

Written by
Heather Bass

Illustrated by
Michaela Robertson

Book design, formatting, & publication services
donated by

www.redribbitreads.com
@redribbitreads

Library of Congress Control Number: 2023903080

ISBN (paperback) 978-1-960622-00-6
ISBN (hardback) 978-1-960622-01-3
ISBN (eBook) 978-1-960622-02-0

Hello there! My name is Grayson, and do I have a story to tell you!

I may be a mature and well behaved french bulldog (well, most days), but ...

I was once just a puppy ...

My first family was so excited to get me.

I was excited too!

After I started to grow, my family was not so excited anymore.

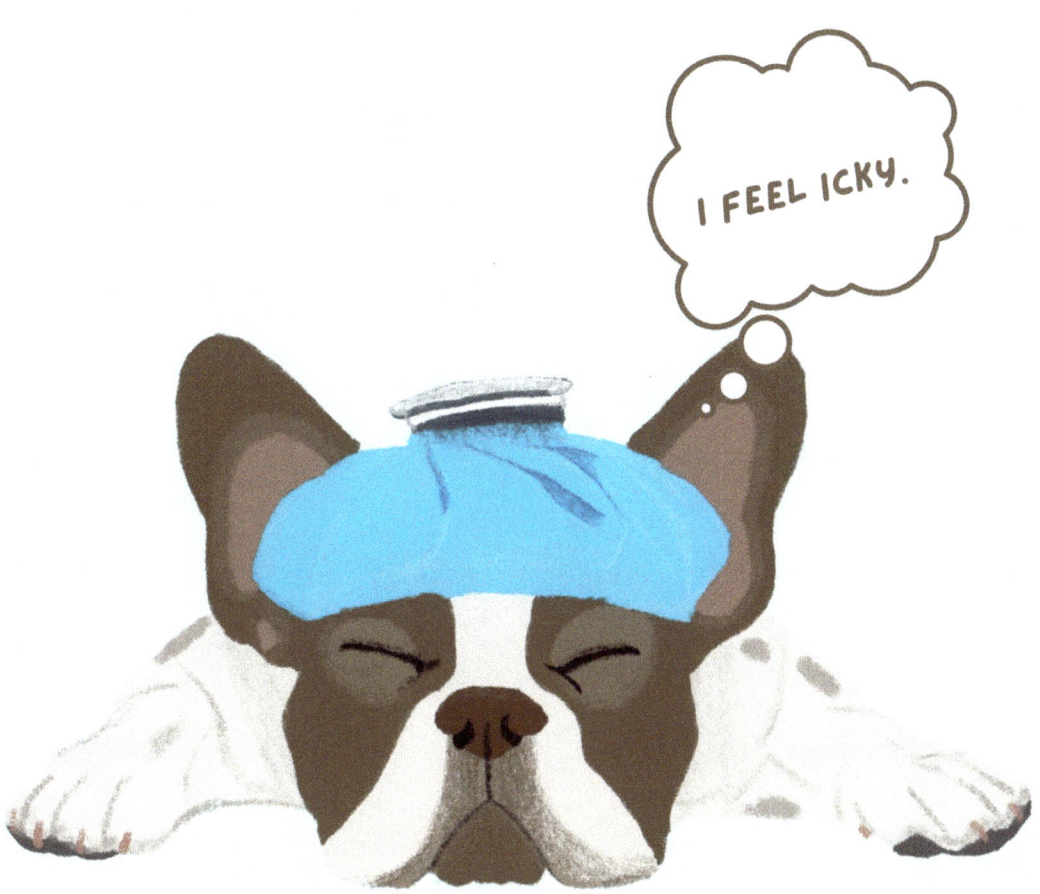

They stopped taking care of me, and I became really sick.

One day, my family took me to a new place.

It was called the

I was so scared and lonely. I didn't know what was happening to me.

I just kept hearing the humans talk about me:

But that day, my life
changed forever!

This new human scooped
me up - big belly and all -
and I just knew...

I had found my

special human.

I was scared during
the car ride ...

... but I loved watching out
the window.

All I knew was
that I felt

F-R-E-E.

We arrived at my brand new house.

Oh, the new smells!

Oh, the new dogs!

I met a dog named Bleu.

I didn't know it yet, but Bleu would become my best friend.

After a good night's sleep, we got up and went to the "doggie doctor" ...

I can't really remember what happened, but my new human stayed with me the whole time!

She did not leave me, and afterwards, she took me back home.

The next day, after a good breakfast and some yucky medicine, my new human said

"Today, We start Grayson's bucket list!"

And so, the

A-M-A-Z-I-N-G

fun began!

We went to the B-E-A-C-H!
Oh, the sand in my paws and the smell of salt in the air!

Little creatures were running everywhere!

I rode in a car with no top! They called it a

C-O-N-V-E-R-T-I-B-L-E!

I also got to stop for a little snack called a

P-U-P-P-A-C-I-N-O!

My nose said
NO THANK YOU!

I had a
professional
photoshoot!

I did get tired from all of the smiling, but hey, I felt pretty famous!

I went to a farm!
You should have seen this
H-U-G-E dog
(well, they called it a C-O-W).

Just when I thought life couldn't get any better, my new human said,

"Let's get dressed! It's going to be a special night!"

It was hard to decide what to wear. I have sweaters that people have sent from all over the world!

They keep me warm, but I think people send them because I am so cute in them.

Our special night had a lot of people, and A LOT of dogs (and by dogs, I mean pugs!)

WHERE IS GRAYSON?

I NEED GRAYSON KISSES!

PUGS ON THE BAYOU

IS GRAYSON FAMOUS?

I MEAN, MAYBE A LITTLE.

Sooooo many people knew me and wanted hugs and kisses.

Suddenly, it got really quiet, and I heard

"Grayson is our king!"

As they placed the crown on my head, I felt like the most special dog in the world!

My human cried happy tears.

When I got home, everyone was so excited to see me!

I went to sleep with a big smile on my face (in my human's bed).

Days turned into weeks, weeks turned into months, and before I knew it, it was my 1-year

A-N-N-I-V-E-R-S-A-R-Y!

Even though my belly has gotten smaller, my human says I am still sick. But, I have a lot of life left in me!

SHHHHHHHHH!

(I really don't feel sick anymore, but don't tell my humans - I love sleeping in their bed!)

My new humans saved me,
with help from so many
others, and a very special
rescue.

I now call my new

MOM AND DAD.

Because so many
people love me,
including my Mom and
Dad, I decided to say
thank you by giving
away kisses to
everyone!

LIVING THE DREAM.

THE END.

About Heartworm Disease

- Heartworms are spread by infected mosquitos.

- They are caused by foot-long worms that live in the heart, lungs, and blood vessels of affected pets.

- Only 2 out of 5 dogs are on preventative medications.

- The cost to treat heartworms is 10-15 times more than the cost to prevent them.

- Heartworms are deadly! They can cause severe lung disease, heart failure, and damage to other organs.

Pughearts
Houston Pug Rescue
www.pughearts.com

PugHearts of Houston

- PugHearts is a non-profit rescue dedicated to giving unwanted and neglected pugs a second chance.

- It is staffed by a network of volunteers in and around the greater Houston, TX area.

- PugHearts has successfully rescued over 4000 dogs since February 2007.

- Dogs are available for adoption year around. There is never a bad time to become approved to adopt or foster.

- To support PugHearts of Houston beyond the purchase of this book, scan the QR code to make a one-time or recurring donation:

To learn more about our non-profit, please visit: www.pughearts.com.

Meet the Author & Illustrator Duo

To simply put it, they love dogs! Heather and Michaela have a passion and love for dogs and organizations that help them. While both have full time careers in the technology industry, they find peace and joy in being able to help fur babies.

With this passion, they decided to write and illustrate a very special story about the journey of a very special dog, the family that rescued him and the organization which made it all possible.

Their goal is to raise awareness about preventable diseases and money to allow the amazing organization of PugHearts of Houston to continue on their mission of "Any Pug, At Any Age, In Any Condition, Anytime."

Heather and Michaela hope you enjoy this amazing story which commemorates Grayson's truly incredible journey.

Did you PUG-HEART Grayson's Story?

Please consider leaving us a review on Amazon! Every review helps drive additional interest in our book, which will ultimately help to support our mission to contribute to PugHearts.

Use the QR code above to share the love!